I0423792

Contents

Research and Evaluation on Radicalization to Violent Extremism in the United States
(CFDA No. 16.560)

Overview

With this solicitation, NIJ seeks applications for research on radicalization to violent extremism as it occurs in the United States, and for evaluation of promising practices to prevent or mitigate radicalization in U.S. communities. This research will supplement work that NIJ funded in FY12, and projects now underway at other Federal agencies. The goal of this research is to aid State, local, and tribal criminal justice agencies and their attendant communities in implementing programs that prevent or counter radicalization to violent extremism. This solicitation focuses on all forms of radicalization that lead to violent extremism in the United States. Proposals should develop and analyze information and data that have clear implications for criminal justice in the following focus areas: (1) comparative analysis at the individual (micro-) level; (2) online radicalization to violent extremism; and (3) evaluations of promising practices to prevent or mitigate radicalization.

Authorizing Legislation: Title I of the Omnibus Crime Control and Safe Streets Act of 1968 (sections 201 and 202), and the Continuing Appropriations Resolution, 2013.

Deadlines: Registration and Application

Applicants must register with Grants.gov in order to submit an application. OJP encourages applicants to **register several weeks before** the application submission deadline. In addition, OJP urges applicants to submit applications 72 hours prior to the application due date. The deadline to apply for funding under this announcement is 11:59 p.m. eastern time on **June 5, 2013**. See "How to Apply" on page 23 for details.

Eligibility

Refer to the title page for eligibility under this program.

Project-Specific Information

In its appropriation for Fiscal Year 2012, Congress provided funds to NIJ for "research targeted toward developing a better understanding of the domestic radicalization phenomenon, and advancing evidence-based strategies for effective intervention and prevention." A subsequent solicitation calling for research in this area (see www.ncjrs.gov/pdffiles1/nij/sl001009.pdf) led to six research awards (see http://nij.gov/dr-projects.htm).

This solicitation seeks to support improving the understanding of domestic radicalization in the United States through the application of scientific research.

Context: Applicants should familiarize themselves with how the Federal government supports and empowers American communities and their local partners to fight radicalization to violent extremism by reviewing two documents released in 2011: (1) *National Strategy for Empowering Local Partners to Prevent Violent Extremism in the United States* (available at: www.whitehouse.gov/sites/default/files/empowering_local_partners.pdf); and (2) its *Strategic Implementation Plan* (available at: www.whitehouse.gov/sites/default/files/sip-final.pdf).

Definitions: For the purposes of this solicitation, radicalization is the process by which individuals enter into violent extremism. Violent extremists are those individuals who support or commit ideologically motivated violence to further political, social, or religious goals. Further, for the purposes of this solicitation, "domestic radicalization" will limit applicants to focus on radicalization as it occurs in the United States, regardless of the locale of violent extremism that ensues from radicalization. While applicants are encouraged to use comparative approaches in their applications where warranted, applications must focus their findings on how radicalization occurs within the United States.

Coordination With Existing Studies: Given the whole-of-government approach that the United States government has adopted to address domestic radicalization and to counter violent extremism, applicants are strongly encouraged to familiarize themselves with research projects that are addressing radicalization at other Federal agencies, including but not limited to the U.S. Department of Justice's Office of Community-Oriented Police Services (COPS), the Department of Homeland Security's Office of Science and Technology, and the Department of Defense. NIJ will take into consideration how applicants demonstrate that their proposals replicate previous studies in ways that build on existing or published research on domestic radicalization when appropriate. NIJ will also coordinate with other Federal agencies to ensure awards are not made under this solicitation for research that duplicates existing studies.

Research Issues and Questions: This solicitation seeks proposals for projects that will primarily benefit criminal justice agencies and their attendant communities at the State, local, and tribal levels. Responses to this solicitation can include explanatory models and hypothesis testing, empirical designs with control groups, thick description, case studies, and other scientific contributions to understanding domestic radicalization to violent extremism as it occurs in the United States.

The applications that NIJ seeks on domestic radicalization should respond to at least one of the following areas of focus:

1. **Comparative Analysis at the Individual (Micro-) Level.** A number of studies have anecdotally compared individuals who radicalize to violent extremism to those who engage in mass casualty violence (e.g. apolitical mass shootings).[1] NIJ is interested to learn more about the operation of radicalization to violent extremism at the individual level. In particular, NIJ is interested in studies that compare cases of single actor violent extremism, lone wolf violent extremism, and mass casualty violence that does not meet the definition of violent extremism stated earlier (e.g. mass shootings in the United States). A single actor violent extremist is one who either "carries out the terror act alone but under instruction" or "carries out the act on his/her own initiative but has previously been in contact to terror groups and/or radical environments" to receive

---

[1] See Petter Nesser, "Research Note: Single Actor Terrorism: Scope, Characteristics and Explanations," *Perspectives on Terrorism*, 6(6), December 2012. Available: www.terrorismanalysts.com/pt/index.php/pot.

4

planning or material support.[2] By contrast, lone wolves are generally considered to be violent extremists that neither have ties to a violent extremist group nor any material assistance from a group, but rather engage in violence in support of a group and/or ideology. [3]

Studies addressing this focus area should consider three factors when designing their studies:

First, NIJ is interested to learn more about these three types of individuals through comparative analyses. While studies should deliver descriptive analysis of cases and trend analysis to the degree possible, NIJ is particularly interested in comparative studies that focus on the role of causal factors in the perpetration of these crimes, including but not limited to:

- The mental health of the individual.
- The ideology to which the individual adheres.
- The role of the Internet and other forms of social media (NB: In the context of lone actors only, and thus irrespective of focus area 2 below).[4]

Second, NIJ is interested to learn where overlaps exist among the three types of actors, particularly in terms of their method or process of radicalization and other analytical factors at the discretion of the applicant.

Third, NIJ is interested in the role criminal justice agencies and other community institutions have in preventing these forms of crime.

Applicants are strongly encouraged to frame how their studies will advance preventative, community-level initiatives to which criminal justice agencies play a significant but not exclusive role.

2. **Online Radicalization to Violent Extremism.** Practitioners are paying increasing attention to the role that the Internet and online social media play in radicalization to violent extremism.[5] Studies and articles addressing online radicalization are therefore starting to follow suit.[6] NIJ is interested in exploring the role that Internet-based or other communication technology plays in radicalization to violent extremism in the United States. The most pertinent questions include but are not limited to:

---

[2] Center for Terror Analysis (CTA), "The Threat from Solo Terrorism and Lone Wolf Terrorism," April 2011. Available: www.pet.dk/~/media/Engelsk/the_threat_from_solo_terrorism_and_lone_wolf_terrorism_-_engelsk_version_pdf.ashx.

[3] Ramon Spaaij, *Understanding Lone Wolf Terrorism* (Melbourne: Springer), 2012.

[4] For example, see Gabriel Weimann, "Lone Wolves in Cyberspace," *Journal of Terrorism Research*, 3(2: 75-90), Autumn 2012.

[5] See Quintan Wiktorowicz, "Working to Counter Online Radicalization to Violence in the United States," 5 February 2013. Available: goo.gl/dRkWH.

[6] For example, see Robin Thompson, "Radicalization and the Use of Social Media," *Journal of Strategic Security*, 4(4: 167-190), 2011.

- What types of online communication technologies do violent extremists most favor, for what purposes generally, and which have the most "impact" on radicalization processes?
- What role does technology play in providing or fostering specific grievances for radicalization, and how does technology use differ across the range of grievances that drive radicalization to violent extremism?
- How does technology and social media advance a radicalized individual or group towards violence?
- Does technology and information technology provide material support to see a violent act through to fruition?

Comparative studies and control groups are strongly encouraged for this focus area, but NIJ will evaluate all applications without prejudice to the method employed.

3. **Evaluations of Promising Practices.** Very few studies have scientifically evaluated community-level efforts to prevent radicalization. Such practices include but are not limited to engagement, outreach, community organization, and educational programs. Likewise, the topic of de-radicalization of violent extremists is a topic of significant interest to the practitioner community, but one that has not undergone the scrutiny of evaluation. NIJ seeks applications to identify promising practices for evaluation. Applicants should identify community-level programs designed to prevent radicalization from occurring, or programs that seek to reform or de-radicalize violent extremists. Ideally, applicants would perform both impact and process evaluations, thereby demonstrating not only "what works" but also the "transferability" of practices to other domestic communities.

Goals, Objectives, and Deliverables

The goal of this research program is to provide a more comprehensive and extensive understanding of domestic radicalization as it occurs in the United States, and to provide State, local, and tribal criminal justice agencies evidence-based tools to address it. The primary objective of this solicitation is to produce research studies that improve this understanding by filling gaps in the existing research or expanding on existing work to provide insights for criminal justice agencies. The secondary objective of this solicitation is to provide the empirical basis upon which to formulate and implement policies and programs designed to address domestic radicalization in the United States. The deliverables from this solicitation will consist of research studies and published works that speak to these objectives.

Evidence-based Programs or Practices

OJP places a strong emphasis on the use of data and evidence in policymaking and program development in criminal justice. OJP is committed to:

- Improving the quantity and quality of evidence OJP generates.
- Integrating evidence into program, practice, and policy decisions within OJP and the field.
- Improving the translation of evidence into practice.

OJP considers programs and practices to be evidence-based when their effectiveness has been demonstrated by causal evidence, generally obtained through one or more outcome evaluations. Causal evidence documents a relationship between an activity or intervention (including technology) and its intended outcome, including measuring the direction and size of a change, and the extent to which a change may be attributed to the activity or intervention. Causal evidence depends on the use of scientific methods to rule out, to the extent possible, alternative explanations for the documented change. The strength of causal evidence, based on the factors described above, will influence the degree to which OJP considers a program or practice to be evidence based. OJP's CrimeSolutions.gov is one resource that applicants may use to find information about evidence-based programs in criminal justice, juvenile justice, and crime victim services.

Amount and length of awards: NIJ anticipates that up to a total of $2,500,000 may become available for between 3 and 5 awards made through this solicitation. **All awards are subject to the availability of appropriated funds and to any modifications or additional requirements that may be imposed by law.**

Applicants should be aware that the total period for an award ordinarily will not exceed 3 years.

Evaluation research: Within applications proposing evaluation research, funding priority will be given to experimental research designs that use random selection and assignment of participants to experimental and control conditions. When randomized designs are not feasible, priority will be given to quasi-experimental designs that include contemporary procedures such as Propensity Score Matching or Regression Discontinuity Design to address selection bias in evaluating outcomes and impacts.

Evaluations that also include measurements of program fidelity and implementation as part of a thorough process assessment are desirable. Measurements of program fidelity should be included as part of an assessment of program processes and operations to ensure that policies, programs, and technologies are implemented as designed. As one aspect of a comprehensive evaluation, assessments of program processes should include objective measurements and qualitative observations of programs as they are actually implemented and of services that are delivered. These may include assessment of such aspects as adherence to program content and protocol, quantity and duration, quality of delivery, and participant responsiveness.

Proposed evaluation research designs with multiple units of analysis and multiple measurements will also be given priority. Design aspects that contribute to the validity of results are necessary to effectively address issues of generalizability and representativeness of findings.

Finally, applications that include cost/benefit analysis will be given priority. NIJ views cost/benefit analysis as an effective way to communicate and disseminate findings from evaluation research.

Please note: All applicants under this solicitation must comply with Department of Justice regulations on confidentiality and human subjects' protection. See "Other Requirements for OJP Applications" at www.ojp.usdoj.gov/funding/other_requirements.htm.

OMB No. 1121-0329
Approval Expires 02/28/2013

NIJ-2013-3489

What will not be funded:

1. Provision of training or direct service.
2. Proposals primarily to purchase equipment, materials, or supplies. (Your budget may include these items if they are necessary to conduct applied research, development, demonstration, evaluation, or analysis.)
3. Work that will be funded under another specific solicitation.
4. Proposals that do not contain a research component or do not respond to the specific goals of this solicitation.
5. Proposals that do not focus on radicalization as it occurs within the United States.
6. Proposals that duplicate existing research or otherwise ongoing Federally-funded research projects. Applicants should discuss how their studies replicate or advance from prior studies where applicable.

Budget Information

Limitation on Use of Award Funds for Employee Compensation; Waiver

With respect to any award of more than $250,000 made under this solicitation, recipients may not use federal funds to pay total cash compensation (salary plus cash bonuses) to any employee of the award recipient at a rate that exceeds 110% of the maximum annual salary payable to a member of the Federal Government's Senior Executive Service (SES) at an agency with a Certified SES Performance Appraisal System for that year. The 2012 salary table for SES employees is available at www.opm.gov/oca/12tables/indexSES.asp. **Note:** A recipient may compensate an employee at a greater rate, provided the amount in excess of this compensation limitation is paid with non-federal funds. (Any such additional compensation will not be considered matching funds where match requirements apply.)

The Director of the National Institute of Justice may exercise discretion to waive, on an individual basis, the limitation on compensation rates allowable under an award. An applicant requesting a waiver should include a detailed justification in the budget narrative of the application. Unless the applicant submits a waiver request and justification with the application, the applicant should anticipate that OJP will request the applicant to adjust and resubmit the budget.

The justification should include the particular qualifications and expertise of the individual, the uniqueness of the service the individual will provide, the individual's specific knowledge of the program or project being undertaken with award funds, and a statement explaining that the individual's salary is commensurate with the regular and customary rate for an individual with his/her qualifications and expertise, and for the work to be done.

Minimization of Conference Costs

OJP encourages applicants to review the OJP guidance on conference approval, planning, and reporting that is available on the OJP Web site at www.ojp.gov/funding/confcost.htm. This guidance sets out the current OJP policy, which requires all funding recipients that propose to hold or sponsor conferences (including, meetings, trainings, and other similar events) to minimize costs, requires OJP review and prior written approval of most conference costs for cooperative agreement recipients (and certain costs for grant recipients), and generally prohibits the use of OJP funding to provide food and beverages at conferences. The guidance also sets

NIJ-2013-3489

OMB No. 1121-0329
Approval Expires 02/28/2013

upper limits on many conference costs, including facility space, audio/visual services, logistical planning services, programmatic planning services, and food and beverages (in the rare cases where food and beverage costs are permitted at all).

Prior review and approval of conference costs can take time (see the guidance for specific deadlines), and applicants should take this into account when submitting proposals. Applicants also should understand that conference cost limits may change and that they should check the guidance for updates before incurring such costs.

Note on food and beverages: OJP may make exceptions to the general prohibition on using OJP funding for food and beverages, but will do so only in rare cases where food and beverages are not otherwise available (e.g., in extremely remote areas); the size of the event and capacity of nearby food and beverage vendors would make it impractical to not provide food and beverages; or a special presentation at a conference requires a plenary address where conference participants have no other time to obtain food and beverages. Any such exception requires OJP's prior written approval. The restriction on food and beverages does not apply to water provided at no cost, but does apply to any and all other refreshments, regardless of the size or nature of the meeting. Additionally, this restriction does not affect direct payment of per diem amounts to individuals in a travel status under your organization's travel policy.

Costs Associated With Language Assistance (if applicable)

If an applicant proposes a program or activity that would deliver services or benefits to individuals, the costs of taking reasonable steps to provide meaningful access to those services or benefits for individuals with limited English proficiency may be allowable. Reasonable steps to provide meaningful access to services or benefits may include interpretation or translation services where appropriate.

For additional information, see the "Civil Rights Compliance" section of the OJP "Other Requirements for OJP Applications" Web page at www.ojp.usdoj.gov/funding/other_requirements.htm.

Match Requirement
See "Cofunding" paragraph under "What an Application Should Include" (below).

Performance Measures

To assist the Department with fulfilling its responsibilities under the Government Performance and Results Act of 1993 (GPRA), Public Law 103-62, and the GPRA Modernization Act of 2010, Public Law 111–352, applicants that receive funding under this solicitation must provide data that measure the results of their work done under this solicitation. OJP will require any award recipient, post award, to provide the data requested in the "Data Grantee Provides" column so that OJP can calculate values for the "Performance Measures" column. (Submission of performance measures data is not required for the application.) Performance measures for this solicitation are as follows:

OMB No. 1121-0329
Approval Expires 02/28/2013

Objective	Performance Measure(s)	Data Grantee Provides
Develop and analyze information and data having clear implications for criminal justice policy and practice in the United States.	1. Relevance to the needs of the field as measured by whether the grantee's substantive scope did not deviate from the funded proposal or any subsequent agency modifications to the scope. 2. Quality of the research as assessed by peer reviewers. 3. Quality of management as measured by whether significant interim project milestones were achieved, final deadlines were met, and costs remained within approved limits. 4. If applicable, number of NIJ final grant reports, NIJ research documents, and grantee research documents published.	1. A final report providing a comprehensive overview of the project and a detailed description of the project design, data, and methods; a full presentation of scientific findings; and a thorough discussion of the implications of the project findings for criminal justice practice and policy in the United States. 2. Quarterly financial reports, semi-annual progress reports, and a final progress report. 3. If applicable, each data set that was collected, acquired, or modified in conjunction with the project. 4. If applicable, citation to report(s)/documents.

OJP does not require applicants to submit performance measures data with their applications. Instead, applicants should discuss in their application their proposed methods for collecting data for performance measures. Refer to the section "What an Application Should Include" on page 11 for additional information.

Note on Project Evaluations
Applicants that propose to use funds awarded through this solicitation to conduct project evaluations should be aware that certain project evaluations (such as systematic investigations designed to develop or contribute to generalizable knowledge) may constitute "research" for purposes of applicable DOJ human subjects protection regulations. However, project evaluations that are intended only to generate internal improvements to a program or service, or are conducted only to meet OJP's performance measure data reporting requirements likely do not constitute "research." Applicants should provide sufficient information for OJP to determine

OMB No. 1121-0329
Approval Expires 02/28/2013

NIJ-2013-3489

whether the particular project they propose would either intentionally or unintentionally collect and/or use information in such a way that it meets the DOJ regulatory definition of research.

Research, for the purposes of human subjects protections for OJP-funded programs, is defined as, "a systematic investigation, including research development, testing, and evaluation, designed to develop or contribute to generalizable knowledge" 28 C.F.R. § 46.102(d). For additional information on determining whether a proposed activity would constitute research, see the decision tree to assist applicants on the "Research and the Protection of Human Subjects" section of the OJP "Other Requirements for OJP Applications" Web page (www.ojp.usdoj.gov/funding/other_requirements.htm). Applicants whose proposals may involve a research or statistical component also should review the "Confidentiality" section on that Web page.

Notice of Post-Award FFATA Reporting Requirement

Applicants should anticipate that OJP will require all recipients (other than individuals) of awards of $25,000 or more under this solicitation, consistent with the Federal Funding Accountability and Transparency Act of 2006 (FFATA), to report award information on any first-tier subawards totaling $25,000 or more, and, in certain cases, to report information on the names and total compensation of the five most highly compensated executives of the recipient and first-tier subrecipients. Each applicant entity must ensure that it has the necessary processes and systems in place to comply with the reporting requirements should it receive funding. Reports regarding subawards will be made through the FFATA Subaward Reporting System (FSRS), found at www.fsrs.gov.

Please note also that applicants should anticipate that no subaward of an award made under this solicitation may be made to a subrecipient (other than an individual) unless the potential subrecipient acquires and provides a Data Universal Numbering System (DUNS) number.

What an Application Should Include

Applicants should anticipate that if they fail to submit an application that contains all of the specified elements, it may negatively affect the review of their application; and, should a decision be made to make an award, it may result in the inclusion of special conditions that preclude the recipient from accessing or using award funds pending satisfaction of the conditions.

Moreover, applicants should anticipate that applications that are determined to be nonresponsive to the scope of the solicitation, or that do not include the application elements that NIJ has designated to be critical, will neither proceed to peer review nor receive further consideration. Under this solicitation, NIJ has designated the following application elements as critical: Program Narrative, Budget Detail Worksheet and Budget Narrative, and resumes/curriculum vitae of key personnel. Applicants may combine the Budget Narrative and the Budget Detail Worksheet in one document. However, if an applicant submits only one document, it must contain **both** narrative and detail information.

OJP strongly recommends that applicants use appropriately descriptive file names (e.g., "Program Narrative," "Budget Detail Worksheet and Budget Narrative," "Timelines,"

OMB No. 1121-0329
Approval Expires 02/28/2013

NIJ-2013-3489

"Memoranda of Understanding," "Resumes") for all attachments. Also, OJP recommends that applicants include resumes in a single file.

1. **Information to Complete the Application for Federal Assistance (SF-424)**
   The SF-424 is a required standard form used as a cover sheet for submission of pre-applications, applications, and related information. Grants.gov and GMS take information from the applicant's profile to populate the fields on this form. When selecting "type of applicant," if the applicant is a for-profit entity, select "For-Profit Organization" or "Small Business" (as applicable).

2. **Abstract**

   Applications should include a high-quality "Project Abstract" that summarizes the proposed project in 250-400 words. Project abstracts should be—

   - Written for a general public audience.
   - Submitted as a separate attachment with <Project Abstract> as part of its file name.
   - Single-spaced, using a standard 12-point font (Times New Roman) with 1-inch margins.

   As a separate attachment, the project abstract will **not** count against the page limit for the program narrative.

   All project abstracts should follow the detailed template available at www.ojp.usdoj.gov/funding/Project_Abstract_Template.pdf and the supplemental instructions below.

   The abstract is a critical part of your application, serving as an important introduction to your proposed study. NIJ uses the abstract for a number of purposes, including assignment to the appropriate independent review panel. If your proposal is funded, the abstract typically will become public information and be used to describe your proposed work. The abstract must be 250-400 words and describe the proposed work succinctly and accurately. The abstract does not count against the 30-page limit for program narrative, and should follow this format:

   1. **Goals and Objectives:** State the purpose of the project, the problem to be investigated, and the anticipated relevance to criminal justice policy, practice, and theory.

   2. **Subjects:** If applicable, include the number of subjects in your study and a description of their characteristics, such as age, gender, race/ethnicity, and other pertinent attributes.

   3. **Research Design and Methods**: Summarize how the work will be organized and conducted by including one or more of the following:

OMB No. 1121-0329
Approval Expires 02/28/2013

NIJ-2013-3489

- Describe the methods proposed including a clear timeline, the type of data, collection strategies, instruments, study sites, and other methods or procedures. For an evaluation, clearly describe the type of evaluation (randomized control trial, quasi-experimental design, or process evaluation).

- State the hypothesis and the innovative potential of the research; list and briefly describe the specific aims; and briefly describe the research rationale and the experiments that will be conducted to accomplish each aim.

- For technology development efforts, briefly describe how the technology is to be introduced into practice and any key technology challenges. If applicable, provide an overview of the anticipated commercialization strategy. For technology research and development projects, briefly describe key technology challenges and how they will be overcome.

4. **Analysis:** Summarize the techniques proposed for data analysis. Summarize steps to be taken to strengthen the reliability and validity of the analysis.

5. **Products, Reports, and Data Archiving:** Describe the expected products such as data sets, interim and final reports, and tools or technologies. If applicable, describe data to be archived under NIJ's Data Resource Program.

Permission to Share Project Abstract with the Public: It is unlikely that NIJ will be able to fund all promising applications submitted under this solicitation, but it may have the opportunity to share information with the public regarding promising but unfunded applications, for example, through a listing on a webpage available to the public. The intent of this public posting would be to allow other possible funders to become aware of such proposals.

In the project abstract template, applicants are asked to indicate whether they give OJP permission to share their project abstract (including contact information) with the public. Granting (or failing to grant) this permission will not affect OJP's funding decisions, and, if the application is not funded, granting permission will not guarantee that abstract information will be shared, nor will it guarantee funding from any other source.

Note: OJP may choose not to list a project that otherwise would have been included in a listing of promising but unfunded applications, should the abstract fail to meet the format and content requirements noted above and outlined in the project abstract template.

3. **Program Narrative**

The program narrative section of the application should not exceed 30 double-spaced pages in 12-point font with 1-inch margins. Abstract, table of contents, charts, figures, appendices, and government forms do not count toward the 30-page limit for the narrative section.

If the program narrative fails to comply with these length-related restrictions, NIJ may consider such noncompliance in peer review and in final award decisions.

The following sections should be included as part of the program narrative.

Program Narrative Guidelines:

a. **Title Page** (not counted against the 30-page program narrative limit). The title page should include the title of the project, submission date, funding opportunity number, and the applicant's name and complete contact information (i.e., name, address, telephone number, and e-mail address).

b. **Resubmit Response** (if applicable) (not counted against the 30-page program narrative limit). If an applicant is resubmitting a proposal that was presented previously to NIJ, but not funded, the applicant should indicate this. A statement should be provided, no more than two pages, addressing: (1) the title, submission date, and NIJ-assigned application number of the previous proposal, and (2) a brief summary of revisions to the proposal. This document should be inserted after the abstract.

c. **Table of Contents and Figures** (not counted against the 30-page program narrative limit).

d. **Main body.** The main body of the program narrative should describe the project in depth. The following sections should be included as part of the program narrative:
   - Statement of the Problem.
   - Project/Program Design and Implementation.
   - Capabilities/Competencies.
   - Impact/Outcomes and Evaluation.
   - Dissemination Strategy.

   Within these sections, the narrative should address:
   - Purpose, goals, and objectives.
   - Review of relevant literature.
   - Detailed description of research design and methods to include: research questions, hypotheses, description of sample, analysis plan, etc.
   - Implications for criminal justice policy and practice in the United States.
   - Management plan and organization.

e. **Appendices** (not counted against the 30-page program narrative limit) include:
   - Bibliography/references.
   - Any tools/instruments, questionnaires, tables/charts/graphs, or maps pertaining to the proposed study.
   - Curriculum vitae, resumes or biographical sketches of key personnel.
   - Project timeline and research calendar with expected milestones.
   - Research independence and integrity.

- Human Subjects Protection Paperwork including Institutional Review Board (IRB) documentation and forms (see www.ojp.gov/nij/funding/humansubjects/human-subjects.htm).
- Privacy Certificate (for further guidance go to www.ojp.gov/nij/funding/humansubjects/privacy-certificate-guidance.htm).
- List of previous and current NIJ awards to applicant organization and investigator(s).
- Letters of cooperation/support or administrative agreements from organizations collaborating in the project, such as law enforcement and correctional agencies (if applicable).
- List of other agencies, organizations, or funding sources to which this proposal has been submitted (if applicable).
- Other materials specified by the solicitation.
- Data archiving plan (see descriptive paragraph below).

Data Archiving Plan: Applications should include a brief plan to comply with data archiving requirements. The plan should be one or two pages in length and include a description of the proposed data management and archiving process including confidentiality protections and level of effort associated with meeting archiving requirements. Associated tasks should be reflected in the proposed project budget and budget narrative sections of the application.

In most instances, NIJ requires that data resulting from funded research be submitted as grant products or deliverables for archiving with the National Archive of Criminal Justice Data (NACJD) (www.icpsr.umich.edu/icpsrweb/NACJD/archive.jsp). The purpose of the Data Archiving Plan is to demonstrate recognition by applicants that data sets resulting from the proposed research are required to be submitted as grant products for archiving according to special grant conditions. Along with other grant products, special conditions require that all research data be submitted 90 days before the end of the project period. Some amount of grant award funds is typically withheld for submission of research data along with the final report and other products/deliverables.

The plan should be submitted as an appendix labeled, "Data Archiving Plan." The number of pages used for the plan will not count against the narrative page limit. The plan should provide brief details about the proposed archiving process including submission of these files: qualitative and quantitative data, final technical reports, instrumentation and data collection forms, and the privacy certificate and informed consent protocols including protections for confidentiality (where applicable). The focus of the Data Archiving Plan is to describe how the grant data products will be prepared and documented so as to allow reproduction of the project's findings as well as future research that can extend the scientific value of the original project (See: www.icpsr.umich.edu/files/ICPSR/access/dataprep.pdf).

Specifically, the Data Archiving Plan includes:

- Information regarding data formats (quantitative/qualitative/spatial) and software with which data will be collected, entered into a database, stored, analyzed and transferred. Standard commercial software or software typically acceptable to NACJD should be identified for use in the proposed data collection (www.icpsr.umich.edu/icpsrweb/NACJD/archiving/deposit-nij-data.jsp).

- A description of procedures by which the applicant plans to collect data along with anticipated units of analysis (e.g., individuals, locations), level of analysis and other identifiers for each data file that will be submitted upon completion of the funded research.

- If the proposed research includes collection of information identifiable to private persons, the following should be included:
  - A description of all assurances of confidentiality made to those persons.
  - A copy of the consent form used.
  - A copy of the Privacy Certificate (as submitted to and approved by the funding agency).
  - IRB approval documentation.
  - Any information transfer agreement used to transfer the data with identifiers.

- Any anticipated variable creation, data transformations or scale construction that may be critical to the interpretation or analysis of the data by others.

- A plan for submission of computer programming code or software syntax providing detail on how the data will be processed including any significant treatments of the data such as de-identification, imputation, filtering or weighting.

- A description of the technical documentation (e.g., data dictionary or codebook) that explains how variables will be designated in the data file(s), such as the use of variable naming conventions and variable groups, missing data/value designations, variable and category/value labels, operational definitions and citations as needed for these variables.

- Contact information for the Principal Investigator in the event other researchers should need more information about the study or the data.

4. **Budget Detail Worksheet and Budget Narrative**

   a. **Budget Detail Worksheet**
   A sample Budget Detail Worksheet can be found at www.ojp.gov/funding/forms/budget_detail.pdf. Applicants that submit their budget in a different format should include the budget categories listed in the sample budget worksheet.

   For questions pertaining to budget and examples of allowable and unallowable costs, see the OJP Financial Guide at www.ojp.usdoj.gov/financialguide/index.htm.

   b. **Budget Narrative**
   The Budget Narrative should thoroughly and clearly describe <u>every</u> category of expense listed in the Budget Detail Worksheet. OJP expects proposed budgets to be complete, cost effective, and allowable (e.g., reasonable, allocable, and necessary for project activities).

OMB No. 1121-0329
Approval Expires 02/28/2013

NIJ-2013-3489

Applicants should demonstrate in their budget narratives how they will maximize cost effectiveness of grant expenditures. Budget narratives should generally describe cost effectiveness in relation to potential alternatives and the goals of the project. For example, a budget narrative should detail why planned in-person meetings are necessary, or how technology and collaboration with outside organizations could be used to reduce costs, without compromising quality.

The narrative should be mathematically sound and correspond with the information and figures provided in the Budget Detail Worksheet. The narrative should explain how the applicant estimated and calculated <u>all</u> costs, and how they are relevant to the completion of the proposed project. The narrative may include tables for clarification purposes but need not be in a spreadsheet format. As with the Budget Detail Worksheet, the Budget Narrative should be broken down by year.

Cofunding: A grant made by NIJ under this solicitation may account for up to 100 percent of the total cost of the project. The application should indicate whether it is feasible for the applicant to contribute cash, facilities, or services as non-Federal support for the project. The application should identify generally any such contributions that the applicant expects to make and the proposed budget should indicate in detail which items, if any, will be supported with non-Federal contributions.

If a successful application proposes a voluntary match amount, and OJP approves the budget, the total match amount incorporated into the approved budget becomes mandatory and subject to audit.

5. **Indirect Cost Rate Agreement (if applicable)**

Indirect costs are allowed only if the applicant has a federally approved indirect cost rate. (This requirement does not apply to units of local government.) Attach a copy of the federally approved indirect cost rate agreement to the application. Applicants that do not have an approved rate may request one through their cognizant federal agency, which will review all documentation and approve a rate for the applicant organization, or, if the applicant's accounting system permits, costs may be allocated in the direct cost categories. If DOJ is the cognizant federal agency, obtain information needed to submit an indirect cost rate proposal at www.ojp.usdoj.gov/funding/pdfs/indirect_costs.pdf.

6. **Additional Attachments**

   a. **Applicant disclosure of pending applications.**

Applicants are to disclose whether they have pending applications for federally funded assistance that include requests for funding to support the same project being proposed under this solicitation <u>and</u> will cover the identical cost items outlined in the budget narrative and worksheet in the application under this solicitation. The disclosure should include both direct applications for federal funding (e.g., applications to federal agencies) and indirect applications for such funding (e.g., applications to State agencies that will be subawarding federal funds).

OJP seeks this information to help avoid any inappropriate duplication of funding. Leveraging multiple funding sources in a complementary manner to implement comprehensive programs or projects is encouraged and is not seen as inappropriate duplication.

Applicants that have pending applications as described above are to provide the following information about pending applications submitted within the last 12 months:

- The Federal or State funding agency.
- The solicitation name/project name.
- The point of contact information at the applicable funding agency.

Federal or State Funding Agency	Solicitation Name/Project Name	Name/Phone/E-mail for Point of Contact at Funding Agency
DOJ/COPS	COPS Hiring Program	Jane Doe, 202/000-0000; jane.doe@usdoj.gov
HHS/ Substance Abuse & Mental Health Services Administration	Drug Free Communities Mentoring Program/ North County Youth Mentoring Program	John Doe, 202/000-0000; john.doe@hhs.gov

Applicants should include the table as a separate attachment, with the file name "Disclosure of Pending Applications," to their application. Applicants that do not have pending applications as described above are to include a statement to this effect in the separate attachment page. (e.g., "[Applicant Name] does not have pending applications submitted within the last 12 months for federally funded assistance that include requests for funding to support the same project being proposed under this solicitation and will cover the identical cost items outlined in the budget narrative and worksheet in the application under this solicitation.")

b. **Research and Evaluation Independence and Integrity**

If a proposal involves research and/or evaluation, regardless of the proposal's rating under the selection criteria, in order to receive funds, the applicant's proposal must demonstrate research/evaluation independence, including appropriate safeguards to ensure research/evaluation objectivity and integrity.

For purposes of this solicitation, research and evaluation independence and integrity pertains to ensuring that the design, conduct, or reporting of research/evaluation funded by NIJ grants, cooperative agreements, or contracts will not be biased by any personal or financial conflict of interest on the part of the investigators responsible for the research/evaluation or on the part of the applicant organization. Conflicts can be either actual or apparent. Examples of potential investigator (or other personal) conflict situations may include where an investigator would be in a position to evaluate a spouse's work product (actual conflict), or where an investigator would be in a position to evaluate the work of a former colleague (apparent conflict). With regard to potential organizational conflicts of interest, as one example, generally an organization could not be given a grant to evaluate a project if that organization had itself provided substantial prior technical assistance to that project, as the organization in such an instance would appear to be evaluating the effectiveness of its own prior work. The key is whether a reasonable person understanding all of the facts would be able to have confidence that the results of any research/evaluation project are objective and reliable. Any outside personal or financial interest that casts doubt on that objectivity and reliability is a problem.

In the attachment dealing with research and evaluation independence and integrity, the applicant should explain the process and procedures that the applicant has put in place to identify and eliminate (or, at the very least, mitigate) potential personal or financial conflicts of interest on the part of its staff, consultants, and/or subrecipients. It should also identify any potential organizational conflicts of interest on the part of the applicant with regard to the proposed research/evaluation. If the applicant reasonably believes that no potential personal or organizational conflicts of interest exist, then the applicant should provide a brief narrative explanation of how and why it reached that conclusion.

Where potential personal or organizational conflicts of interest exist, in the attachment, the applicant should identify the safeguards the applicant has or will put in place to eliminate, mitigate, explain, or otherwise address those conflicts of interest.

Considerations in assessing research and evaluation independence and integrity will include, but may not be limited to, the adequacy of the applicant's efforts to identify factors that could affect the objectivity/integrity of the proposed staff and/or the organization in carrying out the research, development, or evaluation activity; and the adequacy of the applicant's existing or proposed remedies to control any such factors.

7. **Other Standard Forms**

   Additional forms that OJP may require in connection with an award are available on OJP's funding page at www.ojp.usdoj.gov/funding/forms.htm. For successful applicants, receipt of funds may be contingent upon submission of all necessary forms. Note in particular the following forms:

   a. Standard Assurances[*]
      Applicants must read, certify, and submit this form in GMS prior to the receipt of any award funds.

   b. Certifications Regarding Lobbying; Debarment, Suspension and Other Responsibility Matters; and Drug-Free Workplace Requirements[*]
      Applicants must read, certify, and submit in GMS prior to the receipt of any award funds.

c. Accounting System and Financial Capability Questionnaire

Any applicant (other than an individual) that is a non-governmental entity and that has not received any award from OJP within the past 3 years, must download, complete, and submit this form.

*These OJP Standard Assurances and Certifications are forms which applicants accept in GMS. They are not additional forms to be uploaded at the time of application submission.

Selection Criteria

Statement of the Problem (Understanding of the problem and its importance)—15%

1. Clear definition of radicalization to violent extremism.
2. Clear scope of study as it pertains to radicalization in the United States.

Project/Program Design and Implementation (Quality and technical merit)—30%

1. Awareness of the state of current research.
2. Soundness of methods and analytic and technical approach.
3. Feasibility of proposed project and awareness of pitfalls.
4. Innovation and creativity (when appropriate).

Capabilities/Competencies (Capabilities, demonstrated productivity, and experience of applicants)—15%

1. Qualifications and experience of proposed staff.
2. Demonstrated ability of proposed staff and organization to manage the effort.
3. Adequacy of the plan to manage the project, including how various tasks are subdivided and resources are used.
4. Successful past performance on NIJ grants and contracts (when applicable).

Budget—10%

NOTE: *The budget should be complete, cost effective, and allowable (e.g., reasonable, allocable, and necessary for project activities.) Budget narratives should generally demonstrate how applicants will maximize cost effectiveness of grant expenditures. Budget narratives should demonstrate cost effectiveness in relation to potential alternatives and the goals of the project.*[7]

1. Total cost of the project relative to the perceived benefit (cost effectiveness).
2. Appropriateness of the budget relative to the level of effort.
3. Use of existing resources to conserve costs.

Impact/Outcomes and Evaluation (Relevance to policy and practice)—25%

1. Potential for significant advances in scientific or technical understanding of the problem.
2. Potential for significant advances in the field.

---

[7] Generally speaking, a reasonable cost is a cost that, in its nature or amount, does not exceed that which would be incurred by a prudent person under the circumstances prevailing at the time the decision was made to incur the costs.

OMB No. 1121-0329
Approval Expires 02/28/2013

NIJ-2013-3489

3. Relevance for improving the policy and practice of criminal justice and related agencies in the United States and improving public safety, security, and quality of life.
4. Affordability and cost-effectiveness of proposed products, when applicable (e.g., purchase price and maintenance costs for a new technology or cost of training to use the technology).

Relevance of the project for policy and practice in the United States

Higher quality applications clearly explain the practical implications of the project. They connect technical expertise with criminal justice policy and practice. To ensure that the project has strong relevance for policy and practice, some researchers and technologists collaborate with practitioners and policymakers. The application may include letters showing support from practitioners, but they carry less weight than clear evidence of the applicant's understanding of how policymakers and practitioners can best use and benefit from the proposed work. While a partnership may affect State or local activities, it should also have broader implications for other communities nationwide.

Dissemination Strategy—5%

1. Well-defined plan for the grant recipient to disseminate results to appropriate audiences, including researchers, practitioners, and policymakers.
2. Suggestions for print and electronic products that NIJ should consider developing for practitioners and policymakers.
3. If applicable, a clear strategy leading to the adoption into practice of any equipment or software.

Review Process

OJP is committed to ensuring a fair and open process for awarding grants. NIJ reviews the application to make sure that the information presented is reasonable, understandable, measurable, and achievable, as well as consistent with the solicitation.

Peer reviewers will review the applications submitted under this solicitation that meet basic minimum requirements. NIJ may use either internal peer reviewers, external peer reviewers, or a combination, to review the applications. An external peer reviewer is an expert in the subject matter of a given solicitation who is NOT a current DOJ employee. An internal reviewer is a current DOJ employee who is well-versed or has expertise in the subject matter of this solicitation. A peer review panel will evaluate, score, and rate applications that meet basic minimum requirements. Peer reviewers' ratings and any resulting recommendations are advisory only. In addition to peer review ratings, considerations for award recommendations and decisions may include, but are not limited to, underserved populations, geographic diversity, strategic priorities, past performance, and available funding.

The Office of the Chief Financial Officer (OCFO), in consultation with NIJ, reviews applications for potential discretionary awards to evaluate the fiscal integrity and financial capability of applicants, examines proposed costs to determine if the Budget Detail Worksheet and Budget Narrative accurately explain project costs, and determines whether costs are reasonable, necessary, and allowable under applicable federal cost principles and agency regulations.

All final award decisions will be made by the Director of the National Institute of Justice, who may consider factors including, but not limited to, underserved populations, geographic diversity, strategic priorities, past performance, and available funding when making awards.

Additional Requirements

Applicants selected for awards must agree to comply with additional legal requirements upon acceptance of an award. OJP encourages applicants to review the information pertaining to these additional requirements prior to submitting an application. Additional information for each requirement can be found at www.ojp.usdoj.gov/funding/other_requirements.htm.

- Civil Rights Compliance

- Civil Rights Compliance Specific to State Administering Agencies

- Faith-Based and Other Community Organizations

- Confidentiality

- Research and the Protection of Human Subjects

- Anti-Lobbying Act

- Financial and Government Audit Requirements

- National Environmental Policy Act (NEPA)

- DOJ Information Technology Standards (if applicable)

- Single Point of Contact Review

- Non-Supplanting of State or Local Funds

- Criminal Penalty for False Statements

- Compliance with Office of Justice Programs Financial Guide

- Suspension or Termination of Funding

- Nonprofit Organizations

- For-profit Organizations

- Government Performance and Results Act (GPRA)

- Rights in Intellectual Property

- Federal Funding Accountability and Transparency Act of 2006 (FFATA)

- Awards in Excess of $5,000,000 – Federal Taxes Certification Requirement

- Policy and Guidance for Conference Approval, Planning, and Reporting

- OJP Training Guiding Principles for Grantees and Subgrantees

If a proposal is funded, the award recipient will be required to submit several reports and other materials, including:

Final substantive report: The final report should be a comprehensive overview of the project and should include a detailed description of the project design, data, and methods; a full presentation of scientific findings, placed in the context of existing literature; a thorough discussion of the implications of the project findings for criminal justice practice and policy in the United States; etc. It must contain an abstract of no more than 600 words and an executive summary of 2,500 to 4,000 words.

A draft of the final report, abstract, and executive summary must be submitted 90 days before the end date of the grant. The draft final report will be peer reviewed upon submission. The reviews will be forwarded to the principal investigator with suggestions for revisions. The author must then submit the revised final report, abstract, and executive summary by the end date of the grant. The abstract, executive summary, and final report must be submitted in electronic format.

Interim reports: Grantees must submit quarterly financial reports, semi-annual progress reports, a final progress report, and, if applicable, an annual audit report in accordance with Office of Management and Budget Circular A–133. Future awards and fund drawdowns may be withheld if reports are delinquent.

Data sets: NIJ requires submission of all data sets (original, intermediate, and final) produced or collected for the funded project, and any artifact associated with the project data. Included with the final sets of data should be the plan outlined in the Data Archiving Plan section of the proposal.

How to Apply

Applicants must submit applications through Grants.gov. Applicants must first register with Grants.gov in order to submit an application through Grants.gov, a "one-stop storefront" to find federal funding opportunities and apply for funding. Find complete instructions on how to register and submit an application at www.Grants.gov. Applicants that experience technical difficulties during this process should call the Grants.gov Customer Support Hotline at **800-518-4726** or **606–545–5035**, 24 hours a day, 7 days a week, except federal holidays. Registering with Grants.gov is a one-time process; however, **processing delays may occur, and it can take several weeks** for first-time registrants to receive confirmation and a user password. OJP encourages applicants to **register several weeks before** the application submission deadline. In addition, OJP urges applicants to submit applications 72 hours prior to the application due date to allow time to receive validation messages or rejection notifications from Grants.gov, and to correct in a timely fashion any problems that may have caused a rejection notification.

Note: NIJ encourages all prospective applicants to sign up for Grants.gov email notifications regarding this solicitation. If this solicitation is cancelled or modified, individuals who sign up with Grants.gov for email updates will be notified.

All applicants are required to complete the following steps:

1. **Acquire a Data Universal Numbering System (DUNS) number.** In general, the Office of Management and Budget requires that all applicants (other than individuals) for federal funds include a DUNS number in their applications for a new award or a supplement to an existing award. A DUNS number is a unique nine-digit sequence recognized as the universal standard for identifying and differentiating entities receiving federal funds. The identifier is used for tracking purposes and to validate address and point of contact information for federal assistance applicants, recipients, and subrecipients. The DUNS number will be used throughout the grant life cycle. Obtaining a DUNS number is a free, one-time activity. Call Dun and Bradstreet at 866–705–5711 to obtain a DUNS number or apply online at www.dnb.com. A DUNS number is usually received within 1-2 business days.

2. **Acquire registration with the System for Award Management (SAM). SAM replaces the Central Contractor Registration (CCR) database** as the repository for standard information about federal financial assistance applicants, recipients, and subrecipients. OJP requires all applicants (other than individuals) for federal financial assistance to maintain current registrations in the SAM database. Applicants must be registered in SAM to successfully register in Grants.gov. (Previously, organizations that had submitted applications via Grants.gov were registered with CCR, as it was a requirement for Grants.gov registration. SAM registration replaces CCR as a pre-requisite for Grants.gov registration.) Applicants must **update or renew their SAM registration annually** to maintain an active status.

   Applicants that were previously registered in the CCR database must, at a minimum:
   - Create a SAM account;
   - Log in to SAM and migrate permissions to the SAM account (all the entity registrations and records should already have been migrated).

   Applicants that were not previously registered in the CCR database must register in SAM prior to registering in Grants.gov. Information about SAM registration procedures can be accessed at www.sam.gov.

3. **Acquire an Authorized Organization Representative (AOR) and a Grants.gov username and password**. Complete the AOR profile on Grants.gov and create a username and password. The applicant organization's DUNS number must be used to complete this step. For more information about the registration process, go to www.grants.gov/applicants/get_registered.jsp.

4. **Acquire confirmation for the AOR from the E-Business Point of Contact (E-Biz POC).** The E-Biz POC at the applicant organization must log into Grants.gov to confirm the applicant organization's AOR. Note that an organization can have more than one AOR.

OMB No. 1121-0329
Approval Expires 02/28/2013

5. **Search for the funding opportunity on Grants.gov.** Use the following identifying information when searching for the funding opportunity on Grants.gov. The Catalog of Federal Domestic Assistance (CFDA) number for this solicitation is 16.560, titled *"National Institute of Justice Research, Evaluation, and development Grants,"* and the funding opportunity number is NIJ-2013-3489.

6. **Complete the Disclosure of Lobbying Activities.** All applicants must complete this information. Applicants that expend any funds for lobbying activities must provide the detailed information requested on the form, *Disclosure of Lobbying Activities* (SF-LLL). Applicants that do not expend any funds for lobbying activities should enter "N/A" in the required highlighted fields.

7. **Submit an application consistent with this solicitation by following the directions in Grants.gov.** Within 24–48 hours after submitting the electronic application, the applicant should receive an e-mail validation message from Grants.gov. The message will state whether the application has been received and validated, or rejected due to errors, with an explanation. **Important:** OJP urges applicants to submit applications **at least 72 hours prior** of the application due date to allow time to receive validation messages or rejection notifications from Grants.gov, and to correct in a timely fashion any problems that may have caused a rejection notification.

Note: Grants.gov only permits the use of specific characters in names of attachment files. Valid file names may only include the following characters: A-Z, a-z, 0-9, underscore ( ), hyphen (-), space, and period. Grants.gov will forward the application to OJP's Grants Management System (GMS). GMS does not accept executable file types as application attachments. These disallowed file types include, but are not limited to, the following extensions: ".com," ".bat," ".exe," ".vbs," ".cfg," ".dat," ".db," ".dbf," ".dll," ".ini," ".log," ".ora," ".sys," and ".zip."

Note: Duplicate Applications

If an applicant submits multiple versions of an application, NIJ will review the most recent version submitted.

Experiencing Unforeseen Grants.gov Technical Issues

Applicants that experience unforeseen Grants.gov technical issues beyond their control that prevent them from submitting their application by the deadline must e-mail the NIJ contact identified in the Contact Information section on the title page **within 24 hours after the application deadline** and request approval to submit their application. The e-mail must describe the technical difficulties, and include a timeline of the applicant's submission efforts, the complete grant application, the applicant's DUNS number, and any Grants.gov Help Desk or SAM tracking number(s). **Note: NIJ does not automatically approve requests.** After the program office reviews the submission, and contacts the Grants.gov or SAM Help Desks to validate the reported technical issues, OJP will inform the applicant whether the request to submit a late application has been approved or denied. If the technical issues reported cannot be validated, OJP will reject the application as untimely.

The following conditions are <u>not</u> valid reasons to permit late submissions: (1) failure to register in sufficient time, (2) failure to follow Grants.gov instructions on how to register and apply as posted on its Web site, (3) failure to follow each instruction in the OJP solicitation, and (4) technical issues with the applicant's computer or information technology environment, including firewalls.

Notifications regarding known technical problems with Grants.gov, if any, are posted at the top of the OJP funding Web page at www.ojp.usdoj.gov/funding/solicitations.htm.

Provide Feedback to OJP on This Solicitation

To assist OJP in improving its application and award processes, we encourage applicants to provide feedback on this solicitation, the application submission process, and/or the application review/peer review process. Feedback may be provided to OJPSolicitationFeedback@usdoj.gov.

IMPORTANT: This email is for feedback and suggestions only. Replies are **not** sent from this mailbox. If you have specific questions on any program or technical aspect of the solicitation, **you must** directly contact the appropriate number or email listed on the front of this solicitation document. These contacts are provided to help ensure that you can directly reach an individual who can address your specific questions in a timely manner.

If you are interested in being a reviewer for other OJP grant applications, please email your resume to ojppeerreview@lmbps.com. The OJP Solicitation Feedback email account will not forward your resume. **Note:** Neither you nor anyone else from your organization can be a peer reviewer in a competition in which you or your organization have submitted an application.

NIJ-2013-3489

OMB No. 1121-0329
Approval Expires 02/28/2013

Application Checklist

Research and Evaluation on Radicalization to Violent Extremism in the United States

This application checklist has been created to assist in developing an application.

What an Application Should Include:

_____ Application for Federal Assistance (SF-424)   (see page 12)
_____ Abstract   (see page 12)
_____ Program Narrative   (see page 13)
       _____ Double Spaced
       _____ 12 – point standard font
       _____ 1" standard margins
       _____ Narrative 30 pages or less
_____ Appendices to the Program Narrative (see page 14)
       _____ Bibliography/references
       _____ Any tools/instruments, questionnaires, tables/charts/graphs, or maps pertaining to
             the proposed study
       _____ Curriculum vitae, resumes or biographical sketches of key personnel
       _____ Project timeline and research calendar with expected milestones
       _____ Research independence and integrity
       _____ Human Subjects Protection Paperwork
       _____ Privacy Certificate
       _____ List of previous and current NIJ awards to applicant organization and
             Investigator(s)
       _____ Letters of cooperation/support or administrative agreements from organizations
             collaborating in the project (if applicable)
       _____ List of other agencies, organizations, or funding sources to which this proposal
             has been submitted (if applicable)
             Other materials specified by the solicitation
       _____ Data Archiving Plan
_____ Budget Detail Worksheet   (see page 16)
_____ Budget Narrative   (see page 16)
_____ Disclosure of Lobbying Activities (SF-LLL) (if applicable)   (see page 25)
_____ Indirect Cost Rate Agreement (if applicable)   (see page 17)
_____ Additional Attachments   (see page 21)
       _____ Disclosure of Pending Applications   (see page 17)
       _____ Research and Evaluation Independence and Integrity (see page 18)
_____ Other Standard Forms as applicable (see page 19), including:
       _____ Accounting System and Financial Capability Questionnaire (if applicable)

OMB No. 1121-0329
Approval Expires 02/28/2013

NIJ-2013-3489

www.ingramcontent.com/pod-product-compliance
Lightning Source LLC
Chambersburg PA
CBHW052028280526
45793CB00005B/1173